Daily Readings From
STREAMS IN
THE DESERT

Given to: _____

On: _____

By: _____

With this special message:

_____

_____

_____

_____

One-Minute Devotions

Streams
in the
Desert

Mrs. Charles E. Cowman

CHRISTIAN ART
Vereeniging

STREAMS IN THE DESERT

ISBN 1-86852-051-9

Material in this book is adapted from *STREAMS IN THE DESERT* with permission from: Dr Kenneth Kinghorn, Asbury College.

Printed in Singapore.

JANUARY

A BLESSED NEW YEAR

The land, whither ye go to possess it, is a land of hills and valleys, and drinketh water of the rain of heaven: a land which the Lord thy God careth for: the eyes of the Lord thy God are always upon it, from the beginning of the year even unto the end of the year.

Deuteronomy 11:11-12

The Father comes near to take our hand and lead us on our way today. It shall be a good, a blessed new year!

TOO LOW

And there was an enlarging, and a winding about still upward to the side chambers: for the winding about of the house went still upward round about the house: therefore the breadth of the house was still upward, and so increased from the lowest chamber to the highest by the midst.
Ezekiel 41:7

Too low they build who build beneath the stars.

HE KNOWS IT ALL

I will lead on softly, according as the cattle that goeth before me and the children be able to endure.
Genesis 33:14

We have not passed this way heretofore, but the Lord Jesus has. It is all untrodden and unknown ground to us, but He knows it all by experience.

TAKING GOD
AT HIS WORD

*Jesus saith unto him, Go thy way;
thy son liveth. And the man believed
the word that Jesus had spoken unto
him, and he went his way.*
John 4:50

Faith is not a sense, nor sight, nor reason, but a taking God at His Word.

NONE BESIDE THEE

Lord, there is none beside thee to help.
2 Chronicles 14:11 (RSV)

Abraham believed God, and said to sight, "Stand back!" and to the laws of nature, "Hold your peace!" and to a misgiving heart, "Silence, thou lying tempter!" He *believed* God.

THE EDGE OF NEED

When thou passest through the waters ...
they shall not overflow thee.
Isaiah 43:2

God does not open paths for us in advance of our coming. He does not promise help before help is needed. He does not remove obstacles out of our way before we reach them. Yet when we are on the edge of our need, God's hand is stretched out.

YOUR PART

I have learned, in whatsoever state I am, therewith to be content.
Philippians 4:11

Others may do a greater work,
But you have your part to do;
And no one in all God's heritage
Can do it so well as you.

SHOWERS OF BLESSING

*I will cause the shower to come
down in his season; there shall
be showers of blessing.*
Ezekiel 34:26

Look up today, O parched plant, and
open thy leaves and flowers for a heavenly watering.

BROUGHT TO GLORY

For I reckon that the sufferings of this present time are not worthy to be compared with the glory which shall be revealed in us.

Romans 8:18

Made perfect through sufferings, as the Elder Brother was, the sons of God are trained up to obedience and brought to glory through much tribulation.

THE RIGHT DOOR

*They were forbidden of the Holy
Ghost to preach the word in Asia.*
Acts 16:6

Beloved, whenever you are doubtful
as to your course, submit you judgment absolutely to the Spirit of God,
and ask Him to shut against you every
door but the right one.

MAKE US COMFORTERS

*Comfort ye, comfort ye
my people, saith your God.*
Isaiah 40:1

God does not comfort us to make us comfortable, but to make us comforters.

THE TESTING
OF YOUR FAITH

*Reckon it nothing but joy ...
whenever you find yourself hedged
in by the various trials, be assured
that the testing of your faith leads
to power of endurance.*
James 1:2-3

Thorns do not prick you unless you
lean against them, and not one touches
without His knowledge.

JANUARY 13

MORE THAN CONQUERORS

In all these things we are more than conquerors through him that loved us.
Romans 8:37

How can we be "more than conquerors"? We can get out of the conflict a spiritual discipline that will greatly strengthen our faith and establish our spiritual character.

ONE STEP AT A TIME

He putteth forth his own sheep.
John 10:4

This is the blessed life – not anxious to see far in front, nor careful about the next step, not eager to choose the path, nor weighted with the heavy responsibilities of the future, but quietly following behind the Shepherd, *one step at a time*.

THE LORD SHALL
APPEAR TO THEE

*And the LORD appeared unto
Isaac the same night.*
Genesis 26:24

Hide thy tempest of individual trouble behind the altar of a common tribulation and, that same night, the Lord shall appear to thee.

SUBLIME FULFILLMENT

And there arose a great storm.
Mark 4:37

No man is made until he has been out into the surge of the storm and found the sublime fulfillment of the prayer: "O God, take me, break me, make me."

HE WILL NEVER FAIL YOU

*O Daniel, servant of the living God,
is thy God whom thou servest
continually, able to deliver thee?*
Daniel 6:20

Be assured, if you walk with Him and look to Him and expect help from Him, He will never fail you.

TRIUMPH IN CHIRST

Now thanks by unto God, which always causeth us to triumph in Christ.
2 Corinthians 2:14

God gets His greatest victories out of apparent defeats. Very often the enemy seems to triumph for a little, and God lets it be so; but then He comes in and upsets all the work of the enemy.

CONTINUE PRAYING

*Men ought always to
pray, and not to faint.*
Luke 18:1

We must continue believing, continue
praying, continue doing His will.

SORROW

*Sorrow is better than laughter:
for by the sadness of the countenance the heart is made better.*
Ecclesiastes 7:3

Sorrow makes us go slower and more
considerately, and introspect our mo-
tives and dispositions.

A TOKEN OF SALVATION

None of these things move me.
Acts 20:24

When the enemy meets us at the threshold of any great work for God, let us accept is as "a token of salvation," and claim double blessing, victory, and power.

CALLED ASIDE

Into a desert place apart.
Matthew 14:13

Called aside –
From the glad working
of thy busy life,
From the world's ceaseless
stir of care and strife,
Into the shade and stillness
by thy Heavenly Guide
For a brief space thou
hast been called aside.

HE IS WITH US

Why standest thou afar off, O LORD?
Psalms 10:1

We may be sure that He who permits the suffering is with us in it.

JANUARY 24

A SIGN

*But the dove found no rest for
the sole of her foot, and she
returned unto him ...
And the dove came in to
him in the evening; and, lo,
in her mouth was an olive leaf.*
Genesis 8:9-11

God knows just when to withhold
from us any visible sign of encouragement, and when to grant us such a sign.

HE WILL EQUIP US

Thy rod and thy staff they comfort me.
Psalms 23:4

Each of us may be sure that if God sends us on stony paths He will provide us with strong shoes, and He will not send us out on any journey for which He does not equip us well.

GO FORWARD WITH HIM

I have begun to give; ... begin to possess.
Deuteronomy 2:31

We fail many times to receive the blessing He has ready for us, because we do not go forward with Him.

A SPIRITUAL LAW

Stablish, strengthen, settle you.
1 Peter 5:10

There is a spiritual law of choosing, believing, abiding, and holding steady in our walk with God, which is essential to the working of the Holy Ghost either in our sanctification or healing.

JEALOUS OVER YOU

I am jealous over you
with God's own jealousy.
2 Corinthians 11:2

For rapture of love is linked with the pain or fear of loss, And the hand that takes the crown, must ache with many a cross; Yet he who hath never a conflict, hath never a victor's palm, And only the toilers know the sweetness of rest and calm.

AS IMMOVABLE
AS A PILLAR

*God is in the midst of her; she
shall not be moved: God shall
help her, and that right early.*
Psalms 46:5

To be as immovable as a pillar in the
house of our God, is an end for which
one would gladly endure all the
shakings that may be necessary to bring
us there!

JANUARY 30

STILL DEWS OF QUIETNESS

I will be as the dew unto Israel.
Hosea 14:5

Drop Thy still dews of quietness,
Till all our strivings cease:
Take from our souls
the strain and stress;
And let our ordered lives confess
The beauty of Thy peace.

REST SERENE

He giveth quietness.
Job 34:29

Of all Thy gifts and
infinite consolings,
I ask but this:
in every troubled hour
To hear Thy voice through all
the tumults stealing,
And rest serene beneath
its tranquil power.

FEBRUARY

FEBRUARY 1

VEILED LOVE

This thing is from me.
1 Kings 12:24

Life's disappointments are veiled love's appointments.

THE SHADOW CONDITION

*In the shadow of his hand hath he
hid me, and made me a polished
shaft; in his quiver hath he hid me.*
Isaiah 49:2

In some spheres the shadow condition
is the condition of greatest growth.

THE HUNGER OF THE DESERT

And immediately the Spirit driveth him into the wilderness.
Mark 1:12

Nothing but the Son's vision can fit thee for the Spirit's burden; only the glory of the baptism can support the hunger of the desert.

THE HIGH PLACES

*I will cause thee to ride upon
the high places of the earth.*
Isaiah 58:14

Obstacles ought to set us singing. The
wind finds voice, not when rushing
across the open sea, but when hindered
by the outstretched arms of the pine
trees.

NOT WITH HASTE

Ye shall not go out with haste.
Isaiah 52:12

We are in such a hurry – we must be doing – so that we are in danger of not giving God a chance to work.

REJOICE IN HIM

He turned the sea into dry land:
they went through the flood on
foot: there did we rejoice in him.
Psalms 66:6

How many there are who can endorse this as their experience: that "there," in their very seasons of distress and sadness, they have been enabled, as they never did before, to triumph and rejoice.

EXERCISE FAITH

Why art thou cast down, O my soul?
Psalms 43:5

Regarding all our necessities, all our difficulties, all our trials, we may exercise faith in the power of God, and in the love of God.

I AM WITH YOU

*Lo, I am with you
all the appointed days.*
Matthew 28:20

HE WILL silently plan for thee,
So certainly, He cannot fail!
Rest on the faithfulness of God,
In Him thou surely shalt prevail.

A DEEP PURPOSE

He answered her not a word.
Matthew 15:23

The silences of Jesus are as eloquent as His speech and may be a sign, not of His disapproval, but of His approval and of a deep purpose of blessing for you.

BE STILL

Dearly beloved, avenge not yourselves.
Romans 12:19

There are seasons when to be still demands immeasurably higher strength than to act.

MOVE STRAIGHT ON IN FAITH

*As soon as the soles of the feet of
the priests ... shall rest in the waters
... the waters ... shall be cut off.*
Joshua 3:13

The reason we are so often balked by difficulties is that we expect to see them removed before we try to pass through them. If we would move straight on in faith, the path would be opened for us.

LAUGH FOR WONDER

Your heavenly Father knoweth.
Matthew 6:32

The tragedies that now blacken and darken the very air of heaven for us, will sink into their places in a scheme so august, so magnificent, so joyful, that we shall laugh for wonder and delight.

THE UPPER SPACES

The hill country shall be thine.
Joshua 17:18

When the valleys are full of Canaanites, whose iron chariots withstand your progress, get up into the hills; occupy the upper spaces.

REJOICE

And again I say, Rejoice.
Philippians 4:4

Let us sing even when we do not feel like it, for thus we may give wings to leaden feet and turn weariness into strength.

FRET NOT

Fret not thyself.
Psalms 37:1

Dear restless heart, be still;
don't fret and worry so;
God has a thousand ways
His love and help to show;
Just trust, and trust, and trust,
until His will you know.

THE FACT OF TRIAL

*Though I have afflicted thee,
I will afflict thee no more.*
Nahum 1:12

The very fact of trial proves that there is something in us very precious to our Lord; else He would not spend so much pains and time on us.

TRUE FAITH

The land which I do give to them, even to the children of Israel.
Joshua 1:2

True faith counts on God, and believes before it sees. When we walk by faith we need no other evidence than God's Word.

FEBRUARY 18

HAVE FAITH

*Have faith that whatever you ask for
in prayer is already granted you,
and you will find that it will be.*
Mark 11:24

It is so human to want sight when we
step out on the promises of God, but
our Savior said to Thomas, "Blessed are
they who have not seen, and yet have
believed."

BEAR FRUIT

*And every branch that beareth
fruit, he purgeth it, that it may
bring forth more fruit.*
John 15:2

That holds the knife,
that cuts and breaks
with tenderest touch,
That thou, whose life has
borne some fruit
May'st now bear much.

NOTHING SHALL
BE IMPOSSIBLE

Nothing shall be impossible unto you.
Matthew 17:20

We may have as much of God as we will. Christ puts the key of the treasure chamber into our hand, and bids us take all that we want.

WAIT PATIENTLY

*Rest in the LORD, and
wait patiently for him.*
Psalms 37:7

Patience takes away worry. He said
He would come, and His promise is
equal to His presence.

BELIEVE

If thou canst believe, all things are possible to him that believeth.
Mark 9:23

Faith adds its "Amen" to God's "Yea," and then takes its hands off, and leaves God to finish His work.

GOD'S OPPORTUNITY

And there came a lion.
1 Samuel 17:34

Every difficulty that presents itself to us, if we receive it in the right way, is God's opportunity. When the "lion" comes, recognize it as God's opportunity no matter how rough the exterior.

UNKNOWN MULTITUDE

*John did no miracle: but all things that
John spake of this man were true.*
John 10:41

God calls many of His most valued
workers from the unknown multitude.

TERRITORY OF DIVINE PROMISES

*Every place that the sole of
your foot shall tread upon, that
have I given unto you.*
Joshua 1:3

There is the unclaimed, untrodden territory of divine promises ... and it is God's will that we should, as it were, measure off that territory by the feet of obedient faith and believing obedience, thus claiming and appropriating it for our own.

HEAVEN TO YOUR SOULS

My grace is sufficient for thee.
2 Corinthians 12:9

Little faith will bring your souls to heaven, but great faith will bring heaven to your souls.

LEFT ALONE

*And Jacob was left alone; and
there wrestled a man with him
until the breaking of the day.*
Genesis 32:24

If chosen men had never been alone,
In deepest silence open-doored to God,
No greatness would ever have been
dreamed or done.

SACRIFICE OF PRAISE

*Let us offer the sacrifice of
praise to God continually.*
Hebrews 13:15

These pains and trouble here are like
the type which the printers set; as they
look now, we have to read them back-
wards; but up yonder, when the Lord
God prints us off in the life to come,
we shall find they make brave reading.

THE DEEP

Launch out into the deep.
Luke 5:4

Its streams the whole creation reach,
So plenteous is the store;
Enough for all, enough for each;
Enough forevermore.

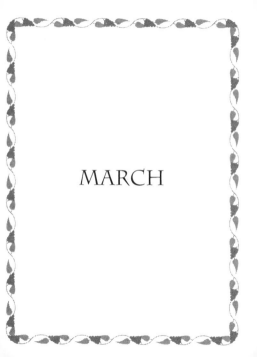

MARCH

THE WORK OF GOD

*Consider the work of God: for
who can make that straight,
which he hath made crooked?*
Ecclesiastes 7:13

It puzzles me; but, Lord,
Thou understandest,
And wilt one day
explain this crooked thing.
Meanwhile, I know that it
has worked out Thy best –
Its very crookedness
taught me to cling.

MARCH 2

A FEW QUIET MOMENTS

Be ready in the moring, and come up ... present thyself there to me in the top of the mount. And no man shall come up with thee.
Exodus 34:2-3

Face the work of every day with the influence of a few thoughtful, quiet moments with your heart and God.

A SORE FIGHT

*And the spirit cried, and rent
him sore, and came out of him.*
Mark 9:26

Evil never surrenders its hold without a sore fight. We never pass into any spiritual inheritance through the delightful exercise of a picnic, but always through the grim contentions of the battlefield.

INHERIT THE PROMISES

*Followers of them who through faith
and patience inherit the promises.*
Hebrews 6:12

When the fire is hottest, hold still, for
there will be a blessed "afterward"; and
with Job we may be able to say, "When
he hath tried me I shall come forth as
gold."

HOLD UNTO THE END

*We are made partakers of Christ,
if we hold the beginning of our
confidence stedfast unto the end.*
Hebrews 3:14

The problem of getting great things from God is being able to hold on for the last half hour.

MARCH 6

I TRUST HIM

We trusted.
Luke 24:21

The soft, sweet summer was warm
and glowing,
Bright were the blossoms
on every bough:
I trusted Him
when the roses were blooming;
I trust Him now ...

MARCH 7

LEARN TO TRUST GOD

We were troubled on every side.
2 Corinthians 7:5

There is no way of learning faith except by trial. It is God's school of faith, and it is far better for us to learn to trust God than to enjoy life.

CLAIM A PROMISE

*Do as thou hast said ... that thy
name may be magnified for ever.*
1 Chronicles 17:23-24

There is hardly any position more
utterly beautiful, strong, or safe, than
to put the finger upon some promise
of the divine word, and claim it.

WINGS OF FAITH

Look from the top.
The Song of Solomon 4:8

Crushing weights give the Christian wings.

LIVE BY FAITH

The just shall live by faith.
Hebrews 10:38

When I cannot enjoy the faith of assurance, I live by the faith of adherence.

MARCH 11

GOD CALLS

*... the Lord, spake unto Joshua the
Son of Nun, Moses' minister, saying,
Moses my servant is dead; now there-
fore arise, go over this Jordan, thou,
and all this people.*
Joshua 1:2

If we turn away from the gloom, and
take up the tasks and duties to which
God calls us, the light will come again,
and we shall grow stronger.

MY TRUSTING
HEART SINGS

*And the Lord turned a mighty
strong west wind, which took away
the locusts, and cast them into the
Red sea; there remained not one
locust in all the coasts of Egypt.*
Exodus 10:19

Though winds are wild,
And the gale unleashed,
My trusting heart still sings:
I know that they mean
No harm to me,
He rideth on their wings.

MARCH 13

OUR GOD IS GLORIFIED

*Just and true are thy ways,
thou King of saints.*
Revelation 15:3

When the fire of affliction draws songs of praise from us, then indeed we are purified, and our God is glorified!

RADIANT WITH
HIS GLORY

*Moses drew near unto the thick
darkness where God was.*
Exodus 20:21

Do not be afraid to enter the cloud
that is settling down on your life.
God is in it.
The other side is
radiant with His glory.

A NEW INSTRUMENT

Fear not, thou worm Jacob ... I will make thee a new sharp threshing instrument having teeth.
Isaiah 41:14-15

He can take the life crushed by pain or sorrow and make it into a harp whose music shall be all praise.

GIVE HIM FIRST PLACE

Give unto the Lord ...
Psalms 29:1

Give of your best to the Master;
Give Him first place in your heart;
Give Him first place in your service,
Consecrate every part.

MARCH 17

PATIENCE AND TRUST

Be thou there until I bring thee word.
Matthew 2:13

Patience and trust, in the dullness of the routine of life, will be the best preparation for a courageous bearing of the tug and strain of the larger opportunity which God may sometime send you.

HOLD YOUR PEACE

He answered nothing.
Mark 15:3

My friend, have
you for far much less,
With rage,
which you called righteousness,
Resented slights with great distress?
Your Saviour "held His peace."

SUFFER HIS WILL

*Beloved, do not be surprised at
the ordeal that has come to test you
... you are sharing what Christ
suffered; so rejoice in it.*
1 Peter 4:12

To wait for God, and to suffer His
will, is to know Him in the fellowship
of His sufferings, and to be conformed
to the likeness of His Son.

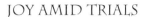

JOY AMID TRIALS

As sorrowful, yet always rejoicing.
2 Corinthians 6:10

Amid manifold trials, souls which love God will find reasons for bounding, leaping joy.

THE FULFILLMENT
OF HIS WORD

According to your faith be it unto you.
Matthew 9:29

No earthly circumstances can hinder the fulfillment of His Word if we look steadfastly at the immutability of that Word and not at the uncertainty of this ever-changing world.

WORTHWHILE WAIT

And when forty years were expired, there appeared to him in the wilderness of mount Sinai an angel of the Lord in a flame of fire.
Acts 7:30

God is never in a hurry but spends years with those He expects to greatly use. He never thinks the days of preparation too long or too dull.

PREPARING US

*Out of the spoils won in battles
did they dedicate to maintain
the house of the LORD.*
1 Chronicles 26:27

Someday we shall find that the spoils
we have won from our trials were just
preparing us ... to lead our fellow pilgrims triumphantly through trial to the
city of the King.

SURE IN PRAYER

And Jacob said, O God of my father Abraham, and God of my father Isaac, the LORD which saidst unto me, Return unto thy country, and to thy kindred, and I will deal well with thee: Deliver me, I pray thee.
Genesis 32:9, 11

Be sure in prayer, to get your feet well on a promise; it will give you purchase enough to force open the gates of heaven, and to take it by force.

HE IS

*But without faith it is impossible
to please him: for he that cometh
to God must believe that he is,
and that he is a rewarder of them
that diligently seek him.*
Hebrews 11:6

When obstacles and trials seem
Like prison walls to be,
I do the little I can do
And leave the rest to Thee.

HEAVENLY HOPE

*Look from the place where thou
art northward, and southward,
and eastward, and westward: for
all the land which thou seest, to
thee will I give it.*
Genesis 13:14-15

He who breathes into our hearts the
heavenly hope, will not deceive or fail
us when we press forward to its realization.

MARCH 27

THE GLORY TO COME

I do not count the sufferings of our present life worthy of mention when compared with the glory that is to be revealed and bestowed upon us.
Romans 8:18

Some glad day, all watching past,
You will come for me at last;
Then I'll see you, hear your voice,
Be with you, with you rejoice;

BELIEVE

And it shall come to pass, as soon as the soles of the feet of the priests that bear the ark of the LORD, the Lord of all the earth, shall rest in the waters of Jordan, that the waters of Jordan shall be cut off from the waters that come down from above; and they shall stand upon an heap.
Joshua 3:13

Let us, today, attempt great things for God; take His faith and believe for them and His strength to accomplish them.

LEAVE IT WITH HIM

Consider the lilies ... how they grow.
Matthew 6:28

Whatever you need,
if you seek it in prayer,
You can leave it with Him –
for you are His care.

WALK WITH GOD

*Behold, all ye that kindle a fire,
that compass yourselves about with
sparks: walk in the light of your fire,
and in the sparks that ye have kindled.
This shall ye have of mine hand; ye
shall lie down in sorrow.*
Isaiah 50:11

Remember that it is better to walk in
the dark with God than to walk alone
in the light.

A SAFE LANDING

The wind was contrary.
Matthew 14:24

Jesus Christ is no security *against* storms, but He is perfect security *in* storms. He has never promised you an easy passage, only a safe landing.

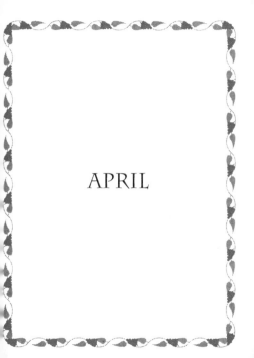

APRIL

COME WHAT MAY

*Though he slay me, yet
will I trust in him.*
Job 13:15

You must stay upon the Lord; and come what may, you must hold fast your confidence in God's faithfulness.

WHEN YOU LOOK UP

*They looked ... and, behold, the glory of
the LORD appeared in the cloud.*
Exodus 16:10

Keep looking up –
When worn,
distracted with the fight;
Your Captain gives you
conquering might
When you look up.

IN TIMES OF TROUBLE

Glorify ye the LORD in the fires.
Isaiah 24:15

A man has as much religion as he can show in times of trouble.

PLACES OF GLORIOUS VICTORY

Elisha prayed, and said, LORD, I pray thee, open his eyes, that he may see.
2 Kings 6:17

This is the prayer we need to pray for ourselves; for the world all around us is full of God's horses and chariots, waiting to carry us to places of glorious victory.

SOME PRECIOUS THOUGHT

*Thou shalt shut the door
upon thee and upon thy sons.*
2 Kings 4:4

God sometimes shuts the door
and shuts us in,
That He may speak,
perchance through grief or pain,
And softly, heart to heart,
above the din,
May tell some precious thought.

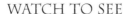

APRIL 6

WATCH TO SEE

*I will stand upon my watch, and
set me upon the tower, and will watch
to see what he will say unto me.*
Habakkuk 2:1

If we ever fail to receive strength and
defense from Him, it is because we are
not on the outlook for it.

"BE STILL!"

Their strength is to sit still.
Isaiah 30:7

Not as an athlete
wrestling for a crown,
Not taking Heaven
by violence of will;
But with thy Father
as a child sit down,
And know the bliss that follows His
"Be Still!"

THE PATH OF PAIN

Therefore I take pleasure in infirmities, in reproaches, in necessities, in persecutions, in distresses for Christ's sake: for when I am weak, then am I strong.
2 Corinthians 12:10

Show me that I have climbed to Thee by the path of pain. Show me that my tears have made my rainbows.

WEIGHTS AS WELL AS WINGS

All things work together for good to them that love God.
Romans 8:28

Let us take the weights as well as the wings, and thus divinely impelled, let us press on with faith and patience in our high and heavenly calling.

SHOW ME

*Show me wherefore
thou contendest with me.*
Job 10:2

God trains His soldiers, not in tents of ease and luxury, but by turning them out and using them to forced marches and hard service.

IN THE
SHADOWS OF LIFE

*What I tell you in darkness,
that speak ye in light.*
Matthew 10:27

Some hearts, like evening primroses,
open more beautifully in the shadows
of life.

TEMPTATION

*And Jesus being full of the Holy Ghost
returned from Jordan, and was led by
the Spirit into the wilderness, being
forty days tempted of the devil.*
Luke 4:1-2

Temptation often comes upon a man
with its strongest power when he is
nearest to God.

RESTING PLACES

And the hand of the LORD was there upon me; and he said unto me, Arise, go forth into the plain, and I will there talk with thee.
Ezekiel 3:22

God provides resting places as well as working places. Rest, then, and be thankful when He brings you, wearied to a wayside well.

THE SUMMONS TO RISE

*For the Lord himself shall descend
from heaven with a shout, ... and the
dead in Christ shall rise first: then we
which are alive and remain shall be
caught up together with them in the
clouds, to meet the Lord in the air:
and so shall we ever be with the Lord.*
1 Thessalonians 4:16, 17

A soldier said, "When I die do not
sound taps over my grave, but reveille,
the morning call, the summons to rise."

AT HIS WORD

I trust in thy word.
Psalms 119:42

Faith rests on the naked Word of God. When we take Him at His Word the heart is at peace.

OBEY BY FAITH

By faith Abraham, when he was called to go out into a place which he should after receive for an inheritance, obeyed.
Hebrews 11:8

Whither he went, he knew not; it was enough for him to know that he went with God.

THE HAND OF THE LORD

The hand of the LORD hath wrought this.
Job 12:9

Not a blow will be permitted to fall upon your shrinking soul but that the love of God permits it, and works out from its depths, blessing and spiritual enrichment unseen, and unthought of by you.

SUBMIT TO HIM

And he shall bring it to pass.
Psalms 37:5

It is impossible for the Lord to fight our battles for us when we insist upon trying to fight them ourselves.

STAND STILL

*Stand still, and see the
salvation of the LORD.*
Exodus 14:13

Do not force yourself to any action.
If you have a restraint in your spirit,
wait until all is clear, and do not go
against it.

ABANDONED
TO HIS WILL

*Not by might, nor by power, but by
my spirit, saith the LORD of hosts.*
Zechariah 4:6

Utterly abandoned
to the will of God;
Seeking for no other path
than my Master trod;
Leaving ease and pleasure,
making Him my choice,
Waiting for His guidance,
listening for His voice.

THE TREASURE HOUSE OF BLESSING

*And being absolutely certain
that whatever promise He is bound
by, He is able to make good.*
Romans 4:21

Climb to the treasure house of blessing on the ladder made of divine promises. By a promise as by a key open the door to the riches of God's grace and favor.

HE KNOWETH

He knoweth the way that I take.
Job 23:10

The furnace is hot; but not only can we trust the hand that kindles it, but we have the assurance that the fires are lighted not to consume, but to refine.

FAITH SEES HER GOD

*Though I walk in the midst
of trouble, thou wilt revive me.*
Psalms 138:7

Fear not that the whirlwind
shall carry thee hence,
Nor wait for its onslaught
in breathless suspense,
For there is a shelter,
sunlighted and warm,
And Faith sees her God
through the eye of the storm.

FAITH IS ...

*Faith is ... the evidence
of things not seen.*
Hebrews 11:1

True faith drops its letter in the post office box, and lets it go. Distrust holds on to a corner of it, and wonders that the answer never comes.

THE BRIGHTEST BEGINNING

*And there was Mary Magdalene
and the other Mary, sitting over
against the sepulchre.*
Matthew 27:61

Where the end of hope is, there is the
brightest beginning of fruition. Where
the darkness is thickest, there the bright
beaming light that never is set, is about
to emerge.

THE PRICELESS PRIVILEGE

*I even reckon all things as pure loss
because of the priceless privilege of
knowing Christ Jesus my Lord.*
Philippians 3:8

Light comes only at the cost of that
which produces it. Burning must come
before shining. We cannot be of great
use to others without cost to ourselves.

I AM ALIVE

I am he that liveth, and was dead; and,
behold, I am alive for evermore.
Revelation 1:18

Turn not your faces to the past that we may worship only at His grave, but above and within that we may worship the Christ that lives. And because He lives, we shall live also.

THE DISCIPLINE OF LIFE

*And when the children of
Israel cried unto the LORD, the
LORD raised up a deliverer.*
Judges 3:9

Let the Holy Ghost prepare you, dear
friend, by the discipline of life; and
when the last finishing touch has been
given to the marble, it will be easy for
God to put it on the pedestal, and fit it
into its niche.

STILL IN THE HEAVENS

*Elias was a man subject
to like passions as we are.*
James 5:17

Let sight give as discouraging reports as it may, but pay no attention to these. The Living God is still in the heavens and even to delay is part of His goodness.

ABIDE IN CHRIST

*And the ill favoured and leanfleshed
kine did eat up the seven well favoured
and fat kine ... and the seven thin ears
devoured the seven rank and full ears.*
Genesis 41:4, 7

"Fresh touch with God," by abiding
in Christ, alone will keep the lean kine
and the ill-favored grain out of my life.

MAY

MAY 1

"COME TO ME."

God that cannot lie promised.
Titus 1:2

The Shepherd does not ask of thee
Faith in thy faith, but only
faith in Him;
And this He meant in saying,
"Come to me."
In light or darkness
seek to do His will,
And leave the work of faith
to Jesus still.

HIS KINGDOM RULETH

*The LORD hath prepared his
throne in the heavens; and his
kingdom ruleth over all.*
Psalms 103:19

It is not safe to murmur at anything.
Thy only safety is, in everything, to
love and trust and praise.

MAY 3

HIS ROYAL "SHALL"

And it shall come to pass that whosoever shall call on the name of the LORD shall be delivered.
Joel 2:32

In vain shall I look for deliverance anywhere else; but with God I shall find it; for here I have His royal *shall* to make it sure.

HIS PEACE EVERLASTING

*He maketh sore, and bindeth up: he
woundeth and his hands make whole.*
Job 5:18

This faith – that life's
hard moments,
When the jarring sorrows befall,
Are but God ploughing
His mountains;
And those mountains yet shall be
The source of His
grace and freshness,
And His peace everlasting to me.

SING CARES AWAY

*When they began to sing and
praise, the LORD set ambushments
... and they were smitten.*
2 Chronicles 20:22

We can sing our cares away easier than
we can reason them away. The birds
are the earliest to sing, and birds are
more without care than anything else
that I know of.

HIDDEN TREASURES

*The secret of the LORD is
with them that fear him.*
Psalms 25:14

God may send you, dear friends, some
costly packages. Do not worry if they
are done up in rough wrappings. You
may be sure there are treasures of love,
and kindness, and wisdom hidden
within.

HIS PROMISES

*He spake a parable unto them
... that men ought always to
pray, and not to faint.*
Luke 18:1

Tarry at the promise till God meets
you there. He always returns by way
of His promises.

IN THE FIRE

Walking in the midst of the fire.
Daniel 3:25

"The cross is too great," I cried –
"More than the back can bear,
So rough and heavy and wide,
And nobody by to care."
And One stopped softly
and touched my hand:
"I know. I care. And I understand."

STEP BY STEP

Abraham stood yet before the LORD.
Genesis 18:22

Do not be discouraged, Abraham grew; so may we. He went step by step, not by great leaps.

STAY FIRM

I had fainted unless. ...
Psalms 27:13

Stay firm, He has not failed thee
In all the past,
and will He go and leave thee
To sink at last?
Nay, He said He will hide thee
Beneath His wing;
And sweetly there in safety
Thou mayest sing.

THROUGH FIRE
AND WATER

*We went through fire and
through water: But thou broughtest
us out into a wealthy place.*
Psalms 66:12

Paradoxical though it be, only that
man is at rest who attains it through
conflict.

STAND STEADY

*All things are possible
to him that believeth.*
Mark 9:23

Keep on believing God's Word; never be moved away from it by what you see or feel, and thus as you stand steady, enlarged power and experience is being developed.

"TRIBULATION WORKETH PATIENCE"

*We know not what we should
pray for as we ought.*
Romans 8:26

Much that perplexes us in our Christian experience is but the answer to our prayers. We pray for patience, and our Father sends those who tax us to the utmost; for "tribulation worketh patience."

INSTANT OBEDIENCE

*In the selfsame day, as
God had said unto him.*
Genesis 17:23

Instant obedience is the only kind of obedience there is; delayed obedience is disobedience. It is a pity to rob ourselves, along with robbing God and others, by procrastination.

THIS I KNOW

*Men see not the bright light
which is in the clouds.*
Job 37:21

I have no power to look
across the tide,
To see while here the land
beyond the river;
But this I know –
I shall be God's forever;
So I can trust.

BEING TESTED

*Fear not, Daniel: for from the first day
that thou didst set thine heart to
understand, and to chasten thyself
before thy God, thy words were heard,
and I am come for thy words. But the
prince of the kingdom of Persia with-
stood me one and twenty days.*
Daniel 10:12-13

The rarest souls have been tested with
high pressures and temperatures, but
heaven will not desert them.

GOD BIDS US TARRY

*And when forty years were expired,
there appeared to him in the wilderness
... and angel of the LORD ... saying, ...
now come, I will send thee into Egypt.*
Acts 7:30-34

So often God bids us tarry ere we go,
and fully recover ourselves for the next
stage of the journey and work.

RELY ON GOD

*I was crushed ... so much so that
I despaired even of life, but that was
to make me rely not on myself, but
on the God who raises the dead.*
2 Corinthians 1:8-9

Trials and hard places are needed to press us forward, even as the furnace fires in the hold of that mighty ship give force that propels that great vessel across the sea in the face of the winds and waves.

HATH NOT FORSAKEN

*And it came to pass, before he had done
speaking, ... and he said, Blessed be
Jehovah ... who hath not forsaken his
loving kindness and his truth.*
Genesis 24:15, 27

The thing I ask when God
doth bid me pray,
Begins in that same act
to come my way.

THE CUP OF SORROW

Shall I refuse to drink the cup
of sorrow which the Father
hath given me to drink?
John 18:11

Open thy heart to the pain, and it will do thee more good than if thou wert full of feeling and devoutness.

COMPLETENESS

*I call to remembrance
my song in the night.*
Psalms 77:6

It is doubtful if a soul can really know the love of God in its richness and in its comforting, satisfying completeness until the skies are black and lowering.

THE SURE WORD

He worketh.
Psalms 37:5

But someone may say, "He worketh," if you have rolled it over and are looking to Jesus to do it. Faith may be tested, but "He worketh"; the Word is sure!

DO NOT GET DISCOURAGED

*At their wit's end, then they
cry unto the LORD in their trouble,
and he bringeth them out.*
Psalms 107:27-28

Do not get discouraged; it may be the last key in the bunch that opens the door.

HIS SET TIMES

For Sarah conceived and bare Abraham a son in his old age, at the set time of which God had spoken to him.
Genesis 21:2

God has His *set times*. It is not for us to know them; indeed, we cannot know them; we must wait for them. Thou waitest for One who cannot disappoint thee; and who will not be five minutes behind the appointed moment.

ENDURING ALL

*I endure all things for the sake
of God's own people; so that they
also may obtain salvation ...
and with it eternal glory.*
2 Timothy 2:10

God's promises seem to wait for the pressure of pain to trample out their richest juice as in a winepress. Only those who have sorrowed know how tender is the "Man of Sorrows."

FOUNTAINS IN THE DESERT

Spring up, O well; sing ye unto it.
Numbers 21:17

Our praise will still open fountains in the desert, when murmuring will only bring us judgment, and even prayer may fail to reach the fountains of blessing.

YOUR SWEET PRIVILEGE

Bring them hither to me.
Matthew 14:18

What a source – "God!"
What a supply –
"His riches in glory!"
What a channel – "Christ Jesus!"
It is your sweet privilege to place all
your need over against His riches,
and lose sight of the former in the
presence of the latter.

VICTORY IN PRAYER

I will not let thee go, except thou bless me ... and he blessed him there.
Genesis 32:26, 29

We will not get victory in prayer until we too cease our struggling, giving up our own will, and throw our arms about our Father's neck in clinging faith.

LIFE'S HIGHEST ATTAINMENT

I have called you friends.
John 15:15

The reality of Jesus comes as a result of secret prayer, and a personal study of the Bible that is devotional and sympathetic. Christ becomes more real to the one who persists in the cultivation of His presence. To know Him is life's highest attainment.

THE REDEEMED

*And no man could learn that
song but the hundred and forty
and four thousand, which were
redeemed from the earth.*
Revelation 14:3

Thy Father is training thee for the part
the angels cannot sing; and the school
is sorrow. I have heard many say that
He sends sorrow to *prove* thee; nay,
He sends sorrow to educate thee, to
train thee for the choir invisible.

A GODLY MAN'S INFLUENCE

Like as a shock of corn fully ripe.
Job 5:26

When the sun goes below the horizon he is not set; the heavens glow for a full hour after his departure. And when a great and good man sets, the sky of this world is luminous long after he is out of sight. Such a man cannot die out of this world.

JUNE

GOD'S DESIGNS

*This is the rest wherewith ye
may cause the weary to rest;
and this is the refreshing.*
Isaiah 28:12

God's designs regarding you, and His
methods of bringing about these designs, are infinitely wise.

WHEN ALL ELSE FAILS

*For Abraham, when hope
was gone, hoped on in faith.
His faith never quailed.*
Romans 4:18, 19

The time to trust is when all else fails.

STRONG IN THE LORD

Let us pass over unto the other side.
Mark 4:35

If you are ever to be strong in the Lord and the power of His might, your strength will be born in some storm.

ALL THAT NIGHT

*The LORD caused the sea
to go back ... all that night.*
Exodus 14:21

There may be a great working in your
life when it all seems dark and you cannot see or trace, but yet God is working. Just as truly did He work "all that
night," as all the next day.

LARGE THINGS

Make thy petition deep.
Isaiah 7:11

There is no reason why we should not ask for large things; and without doubt we shall get large things if we ask in faith, and have the courage to wait with patient perseverance upon Him, meantime doing those things which lie within our power to do.

PRAY UNTO HIM

Watch unto prayer.
1 Peter 4:7

If Jesus, the strong Son of God, felt it necessary to rise before the breaking of the day to pour out His heart to God in prayer, how much more ought you to pray unto Him who is the Giver of every good and perfect gift.

SONGS IN THE NIGHT

Where is God my maker,
who giveth songs in the night?
Job 35:10

What then?
Shall we sit idly down and say
The night hath come;
it is no longer day?
Yet as the evening twilight fades
away,
The sky is filled with stars,
invisible to day.

A MOMENT
OF REAL FAITH

*For every child of God overcomes
the world: and the victorious
principle which has overcome
the world is our faith.*
1 John 5:4

Faith can change any situation. No
matter how dark it is, no matter what
the trouble may be, a quick lifting of
the heart to God in a moment of real,
actual faith in Him, will alter the situation in a moment.

TRUST IN THE LORD

Feed on his faithfulness.
Psalms 37:3

The eagle that soars in the upper air does not worry itself as to how it is to cross rivers.

THE BELIEVER'S GOOD

And we know that all things work together for good to them that love God.
Romans 8:28

In one thousand trials it is not five hundred of them that work for the believer's good, but nine hundred and ninety-nine of them, and one beside.

GENTLENESS OF SPIRIT

*The servant of the
Lord must ... be gentle.*
2 Timothy 2:24

When God conquers us and takes all
the flint out of our nature, and we get
deep visions into the Spirit of Jesus, we
then see as never before the great rar-
ity of gentleness of spirit in this dark
and unheavenly world.

A SAFE JOUNEY

In everything ye are enriched by him.
1 Corinthians 1:5

God may not give us an easy journey
to the promised land, but He will give
us a safe one.

REPOSE OF A HEART

My own peace I give to you.
John 14:27

Rest is not a hallowed feeling that come over us in church; it is the repose of a heart set deep in God.

TRIUMPHANT FAITH

*I have prayed that your
own faith may not fail.*
Luke 22:32

Faith links me with divinity. Faith clothes me with the power of Jehovah. Faith insures every attribute of God in my defense. It helps me to defy the hosts of hell. It makes me march triumphant over the necks of my enemies.

IT'S RAINING BLESSING

*For God hath caused me to be
fruitful in the land of my affliction.*
Genesis 41:52

It isn't raining rain for you. It's raining blessing. For, if you will but believe your Father's Word, under that beating rain are springing up spiritual flowers of such fragrance and beauty as never before grew in that stormless, unchastened life of yours.

STEADFAST CONFIDENCE

My expectation is from him.
Psalms 62:5

Delayed answers to prayer are not only trials of faith, by they give us opportunities of honoring God by our steadfast confidence in Him under apparent repulses.

WAIT IN HIS PRESENCE

And there was a voice from the firmament that was over their heads, when they stood, and had let down their wings.
Ezekiel 1:25

Oh, how much energy is wasted! How much time is lost by not letting down the wings of our spirit and getting very quiet before Him! Oh, the calm, the rest, the peace which come as we wait in His presence until we hear from Him!

DO NOT BE DISCOURAGED

Wherefore lift up the hands which hang down, and the feeble knees; and make straight paths for your feet, lest that which is lame be turned out of the way; but let it rather be healed.
Hebrews 12:12-13

Pay as little attention to discouragement as possible. Plough ahead as a steamer does, rough or smooth – rain or shine. To carry your cargo and make your port is the point.

BROKEN IN
CHRIST'S HANDS

Bread corn is bruised.
Isaiah 28:28

Many of us cannot be used to become food for the world's hunger until we are broken in Christ's hands. Christ's blessing ofttimes means sorrow, but

YOUR WAY

Thine ears shall hear a word behind thee, saying, This is the way, walk ye in it, when ye turn to the right hand, and when ye turn to the left.
Isaiah 30:21

Are you in difficulty about your way? Go to God with your question; get direction from the light of His smile or the cloud of His refusal. The will of God will be made clear.

THE DAY WILL COME

It was noised that he was in the house.
Mark 2:1

If your place in God's ranks is a hidden and secluded one, beloved, do not murmur, do not complain, do not seek to get out of God's will. The day will come when Jesus will give the rewards, and He makes no mistakes.

LOVE COVERS ALL SIN

Love covereth.
Proverbs 10:12

Rehearse your troubles to God only.

KEEP YOUR EYES
ON JESUS

*When Peter was come down out
of the ship, he walked on the water,
to go to Jesus. But when he saw
the wind boisterous, he was afraid;
and beginning to sink, he cried,
saying, Lord, save me.*
Matthew 14:29, 30

Not by measuring the waves can you
prevail. Lift up your eyes unto the hills,
and go forward – there is no other way.

ASK IN MY NAME

*Concerning the work of
my hands command ye me.*
Isaiah 45:11

What mortal mind can realize the full significance of the position to which our God lovingly raises His little children? He seems to say, "All my resources are at your command. Whatsoever ye shall ask in my name, that will I do."

DARE TO TRUST HIM

*Speak unto the children of
Israel, that they go forward.*
Exodus 14:15

Dare to trust Him; dare to follow
Him! And discover that the very forces
which barred your progress and threatened your life, at His bidding become
the materials of which an avenue is
made at liberty.

THAT ANSWER IS – GOD

*For what if some did not believe?
Shall their unbelief make the
faith of God without effect?*
Romans 3:3

Unbelief says, "How can such and such things be?" It is full of "hows"; but faith has one great answer to the ten thousand "hows," and that answer is – GOD!

THE LORD IMPARTS STRENGTH

The Lord hath sent strength for thee.
Psalms 68:35

The Lord imparts unto us that primary strength of character which makes everything in life work with intensity and decision. And the strength is continuous; reserves of power come to us which we cannot exhaust.

A DOOR OPENED TO HEAVEN

A door was opened in heaven.
Revelation 4:1

To prisoners and captives; to constant sufferers, bound by iron chains of pain to sick couches; to lonely pilgrims and wanderers; to women detained from the Lord's house by the demands of home, how often has the door been opened to heaven.

WE WILL BE STRONGER

There we saw the giants.
Numbers 13:33

The men of faith said, "They are bread for us; we will eat them up." In other words, "We will be stronger by overcoming them than if there had been no giants to overcome."

THE RESTLESS SOUL

*There was silence,
and I heard a still voice.*
Job 4:16

As dew never falls on a stormy night,
so the dews of His grace never come
to the restless soul.

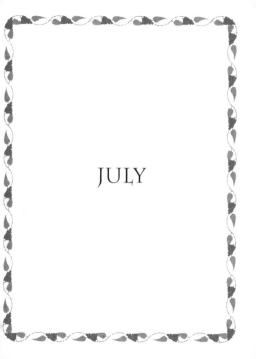

JULY

THE PROMISE OF GOD

There shall be a performance.
Luke 1:45

We must depend upon the performance of the promise, when all the ways leading up to it are shut up. For all the promises of God in him are yea, and in him Amen.

GO FOR IT

When thou goest, thy way shall be opened up before thee step by step.
Proverbs 4:12

Is there a great barrier across your path of duty just now? Just go for it, in the name of the Lord, and it won't be there.

THE LORD'S PURPOSE

Doth the plowman plow all day to sow?
Isaiah 28:24

Why should I start at the plough of my Lord, that maketh the deep furrows on my soul? I know He is no idle husbandman, He purposeth a crop.

AN APPOINTED TIME

*For the vision is yet for an
appointed time ... though it tarry,
wait for it; because it will surely
come, it will not tarry.*
Habakkuk 2:3

Do not grieve Him by doubting His love. Nay, lift up your head, and begin to praise Him even now for the deliverance which is on the way to you, and you will be abundantly rewarded for the delay which has tried your faith.

INTO THE WILDERNESS

*I will allure her, and bring her
into the wilderness ... And I will give
her her vineyards from thence.*
Hosea 2:14-15

We never know where God hides His pools. God leads me into the hard places, and then I find I have gone into the dwelling place of eternal springs.

INTO GOD'S HANDS

Neither know we what to do;
but our eyes are upon thee.
2 Chronicles 20:12

It is such a comfort to drop the tangles of life into God's hands and leave them there.

TRUST HIM TO SHAPE US

He hath ... made me a polished shaft.
Isaiah 49:2

Since God knows what niche we are to fill, let us trust Him to shape us to it. Since He knows what work we are to do, let us trust Him to drill us to the proper preparation.

OUR BURDENS BECOME WINGS

*They shall mount up
with wings as eagles.*
Isaiah 40:31

We look at our burdens and heavy loads, and shrink from them; but as we lift them and bind them about our hearts, they become wings, and on them we rise and soar toward God.

I HAVE CHOSEN THEE

*I have chosen thee in the
furnace of affliction.*
Isaiah 48:10

Fear not, Christian; Jesus is with thee.
In all thy fiery trials, His presence is
both thy comfort and safety. He will
never leave one whom He has chosen
for His own.

NO PRAYER IS LOST

I called him, but he gave me no answer.
The Song of Solomon 5:6

No prayer is lost. There is no such thing as prayer unanswered or unnoticed by God, and some things that we count refusals or denials are simply delays.

FAITH

*It came to pass after a while,
that the brook dried up, because there
had been no rain in the land.*
1 Kings 17:7

Faith puts God between itself and circumstances, and looks at them through Him.

MY BEATEN PATH

He hath acquainted himself with
my beaten path. When he hath searched
me out, I shall come out shining.
Job 23:10

The road you must travel is a pathway of sorrow and joy, of suffering and healing balm, of tears and smiles, of trials and victories; through all of which we are made more than conquerors through Him who loves us.

HE WILL MAKE GOOD

God ... calleth those things which
be not as though they were.
Romans 4:17

Only say you have what God says you have, and He will make good to you all you believe.

JULY 14

BIND US

*Bind the sacrifice with cords,
even unto the horns of the altar.*
Psalms 118:27

Wilt Thou bind us, most blessed
Spirit, and enamor us with the cross?
Bind us with the scarlet cord of re-
demption, and the gold cord of love,
and the silver cord of Advent-hope, so
we will not go back from it.

JULY 15

FAITH INDEED

*This is the victory that overcometh
the world, even our faith.*
1 John 5:4

To trust in spite of the look of being
forsaken; to keep crying out into the
vast, whence comes no returning voice,
and where seems no hearing; and yet
believe that God is awake and utterly
loving; such is the victory that
overcometh the world, such is faith
indeed.

BECAUSE THOU HAST OBEYED

Because thou hast done this thing, and hast not withheld thy son, thine only son ... I will multiply thy seed as the stars of the heaven; ... because thou hast obeyed my voice.
Genesis 22:16-18

There is nothing which God will not do for a man who dares to step out upon what seems to be the mist; though as he puts down his foot he finds a rock beneath him.

BE STILL

*I will be still, and I will
behold in my dwelling place.*
Isaiah 18:4

O waiting soul, be still, be strong,
And though He tarry, trust and wait;
Doubt not, He will not
wait too long,
Fear not, He will not come too late.

NO LIMIT

The eyes of the LORD run to and fro throughout the whole earth, to show himself strong in the behalf of them whose heart is perfect toward him.
2 Chronicles 16:9

There is no limit to what God can do with a man, providing he will not touch the glory.

THIS IS FAITH

The cup which my Father hath given me, shall I not drink it?
John 18:11

This is faith at its highest spiritual success at the crowning point. Great faith is exhibited not so much in ability to do as to suffer.

OUR GREAT HIGH PRIEST

Seeing then that we have a great high priest ... Jesus, the Son of God, let us hold fast our profession. Let us therefore come boldly unto the throne of grace, that we may obtain mercy, and find grace to help in time of need.
Hebrews 4:14, 16

Our great Helper in prayer is the Lord Jesus Christ, our Advocate with the Father, our Great High Priest, whose chief ministry for us these centuries has been intercession and prayer.

SOME SIGN

Let me prove, I pray thee,
but this once with the fleece.
Judges 6:39

At one stage of Christian experience we cannot believe unless we have some sign or some great manifestation of feeling. May God give us faith to fully trust His Word though everything else witness the other way.

SPIRITUALLY READY

And therefore will the LORD wait,
that he may be gracious unto you ...
blessed are all they that wait for him.
Isaiah 30:18

God is a wise husbandman. He cannot gather the fruit till it is ripe. He knows when we are spiritually ready to receive the blessing to our profit and His glory.

IN GOD

*Giving thanks always for
all things unto God.*
Ephesians 5:20

No matter what the source of evil, if you are in God and surrounded by Him as by an atmosphere, all evil has to pass through Him before it comes to you. Therefore you can thank God for everything that comes.

BELIEVING NO MATTER WHAT

Then believed they his words; they sang his praise. They soon forgot his works; they waited not for his counsel; but lusted exceedingly in the wilderness, and tempted God in the desert. And he gave them their request; but sent leanness into their soul.
Psalms 106:12-15

Do you believe God only when the circumstances are favorable, or do you believe no matter what the circumstances may be?

FOLLOW THEE

*What I do thou knowest not now,
but thou shalt know hereafter.*
John 13:7

I do not ask my cross to understand,
My way to see –
Better in darkness
just to feel Thy hand,
And follow Thee.

THE HOPE OF RIGHTEOUSNESS

For we through the Spirit by faith wait for the hope of righteousness.
Galatians 5:5

Thou hast revealed to us that a soul may see nothing but sorrow in the cup and yet may refuse to let it go, convinced that the eye of the Father sees further than its own.

BEYOND WHAT
WE CAN ASK

Prove me now.
Malachi 3:10

I have asked for a cupful,
and the ocean remains!
I have asked for a sunbeam,
and the sun abides!
My best asking falls immeasurably
short of my Father's giving:
it is beyond what we can ask.

THE RICH FRUITAGE

The LORD hath his way in the whirlwind and in the storm.
Nahum 1:3

Fear not the stormy tempest that is at this moment sweeping through your life. A blessing is in the storm, and there will be the rich fruitage in the "afterward."

THE CHOSEN TIME

Hast thou seen the treasures of the hail, which I have reserved against the time of trouble?
Job 38:22-23

The very time our heavenly Father has chosen to do the kindest things for us, and given us the richest blessing, has been the time we were strained and shut in on every side.

ANY KINDNESS

A cup of cold water only.
Matthew 10:42

I expect to pass through this world but once. Any good work, therefore, any kindness, or any service I can render to any soul, let me do it now.

HE GUIDED THEM

*He ... guided them by the
skilfulness of his hands.*
Psalms 78:72

When you are doubtful as to your
course, submit you judgment absolutely to the Spirit of God, and ask
Him to shut against you every door
but the right one.

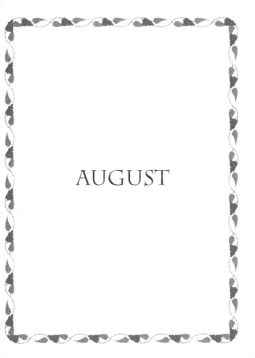

AUGUST

AUGUST 1

SURRENDER YOURSELVES

*Surrender your very selves
to God as living men who
have risen from the dead.*
Romans 6:13

My child, you can trust the Man that
died for you. If you cannot trust Him,
whom can you trust?

A WAY

I will make all my mountains a way.
Isaiah 49:11

The meaning of trial is not only to test worthiness, but to increase it; as the oak is not only tested by the storms, but toughened by them.

BE STRONG

Quit you like men, be strong.
1 Corinthians 16:13

Do not pray for easy lives! Pray to be stronger men. Do not pray for tasks equal to your powers. Pray for powers equal to your tasks. Then the doing of your work shall be no miracle, but you shall be a miracle.

OUR PRAISE

And Jesus lifted up his eyes,
and said, Father, I thank thee
that thou hast heard me.
John 11:41

Nothing so pleases God in connection with our prayer as our praise, and nothing so blesses the man who prays as the praise which he offers.

MY GRACE IS

Is
2 Corinthians 12:9

God cannot make it any more sufficient than He has made it; get up and believe it, and you will find it true, because the Lord says it in the simplest way: "My grace *is* (not shall be or may be) sufficient for thee."

THE NORTH WIND

Awake, O north wind; and come,
thou south, blow upon my garden,
that the spices thereof may flow out!
The Song of Solomon 4:16

The richest qualities of a Christian often come out under the north wind of suffering and adversity. Bruised hearts often emit the fragrance that God loveth to smell.

FILLED WITH THE HOLY GHOST

And when they had prayed, the place was shaken where they were assembled together, and they were all filled with the Holy Ghost and they spake the word of God with boldness. And with great power gave the apostles witness of the resurrection.
Acts 4:31, 33

The greatest question that can be asked of the "twice born" ones is, "Have ye received the Holy Ghost since ye believed?"

CLAIM VICTORY

*Thou art my King, O God: Command
deliverance (victories) for Jacob.*
Psalms 44:4

Fear not, nor be dismayed! The Lord
is with you, O mighty men of valor –
mighty because you are one with the
Mightiest. Claim victory!

GOD AT HAND

*Blessed is the man whose strength
is in thee ... who passing through the
valley of Baca, make it a well.*
Psalms 84:5-6

I have been through
the valley of weeping,
The valley of sorrow and pain;
But the "God of all comfort"
was with me,
At hand to uphold and sustain.

GOD'S UNCHANGING LOVE

When he had heard therefore that he was sick, he abode two days still in the same place where he was.
John 11:6

At the very heart and foundation of all God's dealings with us, however dark and mysterious they may be, we must dare to believe in and assert the infinite, unmerited, and unchanging love of God.

INDULGE IN
A SACRED JOY

Although the fig tree shall not blossom, neither shall fruit be in the vines ... yet I will rejoice in the Lord, I will joy in the God of my salvation.
Habakkuk 3:17, 18

In the day of distress, fly to God; in the midst of all indulge in a sacred joy in God, and a cheerful expectation from Him. Heroic confidence! Illustrious faith! Unconquerable love!

USE GOD'S PROMISES

*Whereby are given unto us exceeding
great and precious promises.*
2 Peter 1:4

Do not treat God's promises as if they
were curiosities for a museum; but use
them as everyday sources of comfort.
How can God say no to something He
has promised?

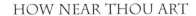

HOW NEAR THOU ART

If the clouds be full of rain, they empty themselves upon the earth.
Ecclesiastes 11:3

O Lord, how near Thou art in the cloudy and dark day! Love beholds Thee, and is glad. Faith sees the clouds emptying themselves and making the little hills rejoice on every side.

ONLY GOD'S WILL

*Thou couldest have no power
at all against me, except it
were given thee from above.*
John 19:11

Nothing that is not God's will can come into the life of one who trusts and obeys God.

THE FRUITS OF SORROW

*We must through much tribulation
enter into the kingdom of God.*
Acts 14:22

The sweetest joys in life are the fruits of sorrow. Human nature seems to need suffering to fit it for being a blessing to the world.

GOD'S HEDGES

In waiting, I waited, for the Lord.
Psalms 40:1

It is a sad mistake for men to break through God's hedges. It is a vital principle of guidance for a Christian never to move out of the place in which he is sure God has placed him, until the Pillar of Cloud moves.

AT HIS WORD

*I believe God, that it shall
be even as it was told me.*
Acts 27:25

If our love were but more simple,
We should take Him at His word;
And our lives would be all sunshine,
In the sweetness of our Lord.

WITH ME ALONE

Alone.
Deuteronomy 32:12

The hill was steep, but cheered along the way By converse sweet, I mounted on the thought That so it might be till the height was reached; But suddenly a narrow winding path Appeared, and then the Master said, "My child, Here thou wilt safest walk with Me alone."

ALWAYS REJOICING

As sorrowful, yet always rejoicing.
2 Corinthians 6:10

Shrink not from the
companionship of Sorrow,
She is the messenger of God to thee;
And thou wilt thank Him
in His great tomorrow –
For what thou knowest not now,
thou then shalt see.

HE LEADS US THROUGH

*And Jacob was left alone; and
there wrestled a man with him
until the breaking of the day.*
Genesis 32:24

God knows how to lead us up to
crisis, and He knows how to lead us
through.

BROUGHT FORTH

*He brought me forth also into
a large place; he delivered me,
because he delighted in me.*
Psalms 18:19

Unto himself! Nor earthly
tongue can tell
The bliss I find, since in
His heart I dwell;
The things that charmed me
once seem all as naught;
Unto Himself I'm brought.

FAITH PERFECTED

And the rest, some on boards, some on broken pieces of the ship. And so it came to pass that they escaped all safe to land.
Acts 27:44

God's promises and God's providences do not lift us out of the plane of common sense and commonplace trial, but it is through these very things that faith is perfected.

IN FAITH GO OUT

*He went out, not
knowing whither he went.*
Hebrews 11:8

Too many of us want to see our way through before starting new enterprises. If we could and did, from whence would come the development of our Christian graces? Faith, hope and love cannot be plucked from trees, like ripe apples.

I HAVE ALL

I have all, and abound.
Philippians 4:18

Among our treasures are such wonderful things as the grace of Christ, the love of Christ, the joy and peace of Christ.

GOD'S WAY OF FAITH

Shut up unto the faith.
Galatians 3:23

Our natures, our circumstances, trials, disappointments, all serve to shut us up and keep us in ward till we see that the only way out is God's way of faith.

CHRIST IS WISDOM

It is not in me.
Job 28:14

Christ is wisdom and our deepest need. Our restlessness within can only be met by the revelation of His eternal friendship and love for us.

TAKEN ASIDE

*And he took him aside
from the multitude.*
Mark 7:33

Taken aside by Jesus,
To feel the touch of His hand;
To rest for a while in the shadow
Of the Rock in a weary land.

BETTER WITH CHRIST

There he proved them.
Exodus 15:25

Happy are we if the hurricanes that ripple life's unquiet sea have the effect of making Jesus more precious. Better the storm with Christ than smooth waters without him.

OUR OWN CROSS

*And he went out
carrying his own cross.*
John 19:17

If we could try all the other crosses
that we think lighter than our own,
we would at last find that not one of
them suited us as well.

THE HOUR OF TRIAL

*They that go down to the sea in
ships, that do business in great
waters; these see the works of the
LORD, and his wonders in the deep.*
Psalms 107:23-24

Remember that we have no more faith
at any time than we have in the hour
of trial. Fair-weather faith is no faith.

IN FACT AND FAITH

*Blessed are they that have not
seen, and yet have believed.*
John 20:29

God has to keep away encouraging
results until we learn to trust without
them, and then He loves to make His
Word real in fact as well as faith.

SEPTEMBER

SEPTEMBER 1

A LIVING STONE

I will lay thy stones with fair colors.
Isaiah 54:11

You are in the quarry still, and not complete, but you are destined for a higher building, and one day you will be placed in it by hands not human, a living stone in a heavenly temple.

ENDURE CHEERFULLY

Unto you it is given ... to suffer.
Philippians 1:29

The richer will be the crown, and the sweeter will be heaven, if we endure cheerfully to the end and graduate in glory.

REST ON HIS WORD

And he saw them toiling in rowing.
Mark 6:48

Be all at rest, my soul,
O blessed secret,
Of the true life
that glorifies the Lord:
Not always doth the busiest soul
best serve Him,
But he that resteth
on His faithful Word.

SHOUT OF FAITH

*And when you hear the sound of
the trumpet, all the people shall
shout with a great shout; and the
wall of the city shall fall down flat,
and the people shall ascend up
every man straight before him.*
Joshua 6:5

Among the many "secrets of the
Lord," I do not know of any that are
more valuable than the secret of this
shout of faith.

WAIT FOR GOD

Blessed are all they that wait for him.
Isaiah 30:18

When we wait *on* God, He is waiting till we are ready; when we wait *for* God, we are waiting till He is ready.

THOU REMAINEST

Thou remainest.
Hebrews 1:11

Through life's days – whoe'er
or what may fail me,
Friends, friendships, joys,
in small or great degree,
Songs may be mine,
no sadness need assail me,
Lord, *Thou Remainest!*
Still my heart hath *Thee*.

HIS PROMISES
TO THE PROOF

*God is our refuge and strength,
a very present help in trouble.*
Psalms 46:1

When God tests you, it is a good time for you to test Him by putting His promises to the proof, and claiming from Him just as much as your trials have rendered necessary.

BE ENLARGED

*Thou hast enlarged me
when I was in distress.*
Psalms 4:1

My soul, if thou wouldst be enlarged into human sympathy, thou must be narrowed into limits of human suffering.

THE DEPTHS OF THY LIFE

Not much earth.
Matthew 13:5

Lord, lead me into the depths of Thy life and save me from a shallow experience!

THE LORD WILL PERFECT

*The LORD will perfect that
which concerneth me.*
Psalms 138:8

The great thing is to suffer without
being discouraged.

WAITING PATIENTLY

And so, after he had patiently
endured, he obtained the promise.
Hebrews 6:15

God's promises cannot fail of their accomplishment. Patient waiters cannot be disappointed. Believing expectation shall be realized.

LEAN HARD

*Who is this that cometh up from the
wilderness, leaning upon her beloved?*
The Song of Solomon 8:5

Child of My love, lean hard
And let Me feel the
pressure of thy care;
Thou lovest Me? I know it.
Doubt not then;
But loving Me, lean hard.

ON TOP OF THE MOUNT

Come up in the morning ...
and present thyself there to
me in the top of the mount.
Exodus 34:2

Blessed is the day whose morning is sanctified! Successful is the day whose first victory was won in prayer! Holy is the day whose dawn finds thee on the top of the mount!

TAKE UP YOUR CROSS

*Whosoever will come after me,
let him deny himself, and take
up his cross, and follow me.*
Mark 8:34

Never is Jesus so near me as when I lift my cross, and lay it submissively on my shoulder, and give it the welcome of a patient and unmurmuring spirit.

FRESH FROM THEE

*Blow upon my garden that the
spices may thereof flow out.*
The Song of Solomon 4:16

Dear Lord,
abide with us that we
May draw our
perfume fresh from Thee.

HIDE THYSELF

Hide thyself by the brook Cherith.
1 Kings 17:3

Every saintly soul that would wield great power with men must win it in some hidden Cherith.

HE IS LORD

*It is the LORD: let him do
what seemeth him good.*
1 Samuel 3:18

See God in everything, and God will
calm and color all that thou dost see!

THE VISION OF GOD

*Where there is no
vision, the people perish.*
Proverbs 29:18

The vision of God always transforms
human life.

THE FINAL OUTCOME

My Father is the husbandman.
John 15:1

Pruning seems to be destroying the vine, the gardener appears to be cutting it all away; but he looks on into the future and knows that the final outcome will be the enrichment of its life and greater abundance of fruit.

THE GLORY OF GOD

*Said I not unto thee, that, if
thou wouldest believe, thou
shouldest see the glory of God?*
John 11:40

Friend, you do not have to understand
all God's ways with you. Some day you
will see the glory of God in the things
which you do not understand.

KNOWING CHRIST

*I count all things but loss for
the excellency of the knowledge
of Christ Jesus, my Lord.*
Philippians 3:8

Plenty out of pain, life out of death:
is it not the law of the kingdom?

FAITH TRIED

*And the Lord said ... Satan hath
desired to have you, that he may
sift you as wheat; but I have prayed
for thee, that thy faith fail not.*
Luke 22:31-32

Faith must be tried, and seeming desertion is the furnace, heated seven times, into which it might be thrust. Blest the man who can endure the ordeal!

RIVERS OF LIVING WATER

He that believeth on me, as the scripture hath said, out of his belly shall flow rivers of living water.
John 7:38

When the apostles received the baptism with the Holy Ghost they did not rent the upper room and stay there to hold holiness meetings, but went everywhere preaching the gospel.

A SERVICE OF WAITING

*After they were come to Mysia,
they assayed to go into Bithynia:
but the Spirit suffered them not.*
Acts 16:7

The Spirit has not only a service of
work, but a service of waiting. In the
kingdom of Christ there are not only
times for action, but times in which to
forbear acting.

HOPE THOU THEN!

Why go I mourning?
Psalms 42:9

Knowest thou not that day follows night, that flood comes after ebb, that spring and summer succeed winter? Hope thou then! Hope thou ever! God fails thee not.

WALK BY FAITH

We walk by faith, not by appearance.
2 Corinthians 5:7

God never gives feeling to enable us to trust Him; God gives feeling only when He sees that we trust Him apart from all feeling, resting on His own Word, and on His own faithfulness to His promise.

THE VERY LIFE OF THE SON

I have found an atonement.
Job 33:24

We are members of His body, His flesh, and His bones, and if we can only believe and receive it, we may live upon the very life of the Son of God.

PEACE IN THE HEART

In me ... peace.
John 16:33

If peace be in the heart,
The wildest winter storm is full of
solemn beauty,
The midnight flash but shows
the path of duty,
Each living creature
tells some new and
joyous story,
The very trees and stones all catch
a ray of glory,
If peace be in the heart.

TAKE TIME TO PRAY

I will give myself unto prayer.
Psalms 109:4

We may lay it down as an elemental principle of religion, that no large growth in holiness was ever gained by one who did not take time to be often, and long, alone with God.

HIS ARM UNDERNEATH

As an eagle stirreth up her nest, fluttereth over her young, spreadeth abroad her wings, taketh them, beareth them on her wings: so the Lord alone did lead him, and there was no strange god with him.
Deuteronomy 32:11, 12

When God puts a burden upon you He puts His own arm underneath.

OCTOBER

TRIALS GIVE BLESSING

*It is good for me that I
have been afflicted.*
Psalms 119:71

The most brilliant colors of plants are to be seen on the highest mountains, in spots that are most exposed to the wildest weather. Trials give brightness and blessing to life.

ASIDE PRIVATELY

*And he took them, and went aside
privately into a desert place.*
Luke 9:10

The soul in one single quiet hour of
prayer will often make more progress
than in days of company with others.

HIS GENTLE TOUCHES

*And after the earthquake a fire; and
after the fire a sound of gentle stillness.*
1 Kings 19:12

He is love, and if you would know
Him and His voice, give constant ear
to His gentle touches.

THE LORD BLESSED

*So the LORD blessed the latter end
of Job more than his beginning.*
Job 42:12

Trouble never comes to a man unless
she brings a nugget of gold in her hand.

OUR HOPE IS IN GOD

*It came to pass ... that
the brook dried up.*
1 Kings 17:7

Whensoever in your life and mine some spring of earthly and outward resource had dried up, it has been that we might learn that our hope and help are in God who made heaven and earth.

GRACE REQUIRED

He opened not his mouth.
Isaiah 53:7

How much grace it requires to bear a misunderstanding rightly, and to receive an unkind judgment in holy sweetness!

SIMPLY TRUST GOD

*Who is among you that feareth Jehovah,
that obeyeth the voice of his servant? He
that walketh in darkness and hath no
light, let him trust in the name of
Jehovah and rely upon his God.*
Isaiah 50:10

We are to simply trust God. While we trust, God can work. Worry prevents Him from doing anything for us.

ABANDONED TO GOD

Do not begin to be anxious.
Philippians 4:6

Worry spoils lives which would otherwise be useful and beautiful. Scale the heights of a life abandoned to God, then you will look down on the clouds beneath your feet.

HIS PURPOSE
IN WAITING

*Therefore will the LORD wait, that
he may be gracious unto you.*
Isaiah 30:18

When thy God hides His face, say not
that He hath forgotten thee. He is but
tarrying a little while to make thee love
Him better.

A DIVINE COMMAND

Fret not.
Psalms 37:1

This to me is a divine command; the same as "Thou shalt not steal."

MEASURE BY LOSS

As dying and behold we live.
2 Corinthians 6:9

Measure thy life by
loss and not by gain,
Not by the wine drunk,
but by the wine poured forth.
For love's strength
standeth in love's sacrifice,
And he who suffers most has most
to give.

KEEP MY JOY FULL

*And Joseph's master took him,
and put him into the prison ... But
the LORD was with Joseph ... and
that which he did, the LORD
made it to prosper.*
Genesis 39:20-21, 23

Lord Jesus, when the prison doors close in on me, keep me trusting, and keep my joy full and abounding.

TO SUCCOR AND HELP

In nothing be anxious.
Philippians 4:6

We have a Father in heaven who is almighty, who loves His children as He loves His only-begotten Son, and whose very joy and delight it is to succor and help them at all times and under all circumstances.

OCTOBER 14

IT IS A MIRACLE

The angel of the Lord came upon him and a light shined in the prison; and he smote Peter on the side, and raised him up, saying, Arise up quickly. And his chains fell off.
Acts 12:7

Difficulty is the very atmosphere of miracle – it is a miracle in its first stage. If it is to be a great miracle, the condition is not difficulty but impossibility.

PERFECTLY BROKEN

*By reason of breakings
they purify themselves.*
Job 41:25

God uses most for His glory those people and things which are most perfectly broken. The sacrifices He accepts are broken and contrite hearts.

REFUSE TO DOUBT

*Let us lay aside every weight, and
the sin which doth so easily beset
us, and let us run with patience
the race that is set before us.*
Hebrews 12:1

We can set our will against doubt just
as we do against any other sin; and as
we stand firm and refuse to doubt, the
Holy Spirit will come to our aid and
give us the faith of God and crown us
with victory.

NOT THEIR WILL BUT HIS

God forbid that I should glory,
save in the cross of our Lord Jesus
Christ, by whom the world is crucified
unto me, and I unto the world.
Galatians 6:14

It was good to suffer here, that they
might reign hereafter; to bear the cross
below, for they shall wear the crown
above; and that not their will but His
was done on them and in them.

OCTOBER 18

HIS NEW COVENANT
WITH ME

*Know of a surety that thy seed shall
be a stranger in a land that is not
theirs; ... they shall afflict them four
hundred years; ... and afterward they
shall come out with great substance.*
Genesis 15:13-14

God is going to test me with delays;
but through it all stands God's pledge:
His new covenant with me in Christ,
and His inviolable promise of every
lesser blessing that I need.

GOD'S HAND

The ark of the covenant of
the LORD went before them.
Numbers 10:33

Where God's finger points, there
God's hand will make the way.

THE PEACE OF GOD

And the peace of God, which transcends all our powers of thought, will be a garrison to guard your hearts and minds in Christ Jesus.
Philippians 4:7

The peace of God is that eternal calm which lies far too deep down to be reached by any external trouble or disturbance.

A TRAVELER

*For we know that if our earthly
house of this tabernacle were
dissolved, we have a building
of God, an house not made
with hands, eternal in the heavens.*
2 Corinthians 5:1

We are all wayfarers, but the believer
knows it and accepts it. He is a traveler,
not a settler.

THE ORDINARY ROAD

Now Moses kept the flock of Jethro his father-in-law, the priest of Midian: and he led the flock to the backside of the desert, and came to the mountain of God, even to Horeb. And the angel of the LORD appeared unto him in a flame of fire out of the midst of a bush.
Exodus 3:1-2

My Father God, help me to expect Thee on the ordinary road.

KNOW HOW TO WAIT

*There hath not failed one
word of all his good promise.*
1 Kings 8:56

Oh for the faith that does not make haste, but waits patiently for the Lord. He has attained to an eminent degree of Christian grace who knows how to wait.

PREPARING US

*I will make thee a new
sharp threshing instrument.*
Isaiah 41:15

Life would be inexplicable unless we believed that God was preparing us for scenes and ministries that lie beyond the veil of sense in the eternal world, where highly-tempered spirits will be required for special service.

ASK IN MY NAME

*Hitherto have ye asked nothing
in my name: ask and ye shall
receive, that your joy may be full.*
John 16:24

"**N**ow shalt thou see what I will do."
(Exodus 6:1)

THERE ALONE

*He went up into a mountain
apart to pray: and when the evening
was come, he was there alone.*
Matthew 14:23

Oh, the thought to have God all alone
to myself, and to know that God has
me all alone to Himself!

DO YOUR BEST

*All thy waves and thy
billows are gone over me.*
Psalms 42:7

Stand up in the place where the dear
Lord has put you, and there do your
best. The grandest character is grown
in hardship.

OCTOBER 28

SAFE IN GOD

But God, who is rich in mercy, for his great love wherewith he loved us, even when we were dead in sins, hath quickened us together with Christ ... and hath raised us up together, and made us sit together in heavenly places in Christ Jesus.
Ephesians 2:4-6

It is your business to learn to be peaceful and safe in God in every situation.

THE REFINER'S FIRE

*He shall sit as a refiner
and purifier of silver.*
Malachi 3:3

Our Father, who seeks to perfect His
saints in holiness, knows the value of
the refiner's fire.

EXERCISE PATIENCE

Let us run with patience.
Hebrews 12:1

Most of us are called to exercise our patience, not in bed, but in the street.

INTERCESSION FOR US

*Likewise the Spirit also helpeth
our infirmities; for we know not
what we should pray for as we
ought; but the Spirit itself maketh
intercession for us with groanings
which cannot be uttered.*
Romans 8:26-27

This is the delicate divine mechanism
which words cannot interpret, and
which theology cannot explain, but
which the humblest believer knows
even when he does not understand.

NOVEMBER

DAILY SUPPLIES

*When the cloud tarried ... then the
children of Israel ... journeyed not.*
Numbers 9:19

God never keeps us at a post without
assuring us of His presence, and send-
ing us daily supplies.

WHO WILL DARE

But prayer ...
Acts 12:5

God is not wanting great men, but He is wanting men who will dare to prove the greatness of their God.

BARE HEIGHTS

*On all bare heights shall
be their pasture.*
Isaiah 40:9

The capacity for knowing God enlarges as we are brought by Him into circumstances which oblige us to exercise faith; so, when difficulties beset our path, let us thank God that He is taking trouble with us and lean hard upon Him.

THE DIVINE WILL

*As I was among the captives
by the river of Chebar ... the
heavens were opened and I saw
visions of God ... and the hand
of the LORD was there upon me.*
Ezekiel 1:1, 3

Submission to the divine will is the softest pillow on which to recline.

THE IMPOSSIBLE

Is anything too hard for the LORD?
Genesis 18:14

Not when we believe in Him enough to go forward and do His will, and let Him do the impossible for us. Nothing is too hard for Jehovah to do for them that trust Him.

I REBUKE AND CHASTEN

As many as I love I rebuke and chasten.
Revelation 3:19

It is not only the grace, but the glory
of a believer when he can stand and take
affliction quietly.

I GIVE THEE BACK

But what things were gain to me,
those I counted loss for Christ.
Philippians 3:7

O Love that wilt not let me go,
I rest my weary soul in Thee,
I give Thee back the life I owe,
That in thine ocean depths its flow
May richer, fuller be.

THEY SAW HIS GLORY

He took Peter and John and James, and went up into a mountain to pray. And as he prayed, the fashion of his countenance was altered, and his raiment was white and glistering ... they saw his glory.
Luke 9:28-29, 32

Here is the world's need today – men who have seen their Lord.

DWELL UNDER
HIS SHADOW

*They that dwell under his shadow
shall return; they shall revive as
the corn and grow as the vine.*
Hosea 14:7

I cannot tell how it is that I should be able to receive into my being a power to do and to bear by communion with God, but I know it is a fact.

HE STEPS FORTH

*Under hopeless circumstances
he hopefully believed.*
Romans 4:18

The most glorious promises of God are generally fulfilled in such a wondrous manner that He steps forth to save us at a time when there is the least appearance of it.

COME DOWN LIKE RAIN

He shall come down like
rain upon the mown grass.
Psalms 72:6

Do not dread the scythe – it is sure to
be followed by the shower.

NOT HALF SO BEAUTIFUL

*These were the potters, and
those that dwelt among plants
and hedges: there they dwelt
with the king for his work.*
1 Chronicles 4:23

The colored sunsets and starry heavens, the beautiful mountains and the shining seas, the fragrant woods and painted flowers, are not half so beautiful as a soul that is serving Jesus out of love.

CHOSEN BY GOD

*I know him, that he
will command his children.*
Genesis 18:19

God is looking for men on whom He
can put the weight of all His love and
power and faithful promises.

IT BRINGETH FORTH MUCH FRUIT

*Except a grain of corn fall into the
ground and die, it abideth alone: but if
it dies it bringeth forth much fruit.*
John 12:24

Is there some desert,
or some boundless sea,
Where Thou, great God
of angels, wilt send me?
Show me the desert,
Father, or the sea;
Is it Thine enterprise?
Great God, send me!

VESSELS FOR FAITH

Pressed out of measure.
2 Corinthians 1:8

When hindrances confront us in the path of duty, we are to recognize them as vessels for faith to fill with the fullness and all-sufficiency of Jesus.

TO WIN YOUR CROWN

*They overcame him by the blood
of the Lamb ... and they loved
not their lives unto the death.*
Revelation 12:11

The very hardships that you are enduring in your life today are given by the Master for the explicit purpose of enabling you to win your crown.

NOVEMBER 17

HIS OWN ELECT

Hear what the unjust judge saith. And shall not God avenge his own elect which cry day and night unto him, though he bear long with them? I tell you that he will avenge them speedily.
Luke 18:6-8

I do not believe that there is such a thing in the history of God's kingdom as a right prayer offered in a right spirit that is forever left unanswered.

NOVEMBER 18

REFUSE TO BE OFFENDED

*Blessed is he, whosoever
shall not be offended in me.*
Luke 7:23

Let come what will come, His will is
welcome; and I shall refuse to be offended in my loving Lord.

HE WILL QUICKEN AGAIN

*Thou, who hast showed us many and
sore troubles, wilt quicken us again.*
Psalms 71:20

Never doubt God! Never say that He
has forsaken or forgotten. Never think
that He is unsympathetic. He will
quicken again.

WAIT

Blessed is he that waiteth.
Daniel 12:12

Wait in prayer. Wait in faith. Wait in quiet patience.

CAST YOUR
CARES ON HIM

*Casting all your care upon
him; for he careth for you.*
1 Peter 5:7 KJV

Roll thy cares, and thyself with them,
as one burden, all on thy God.

IN FULL SURRENDER

Believe ye that I am able to do this?
Matthew 9:28

If in our own life there have been rebellion, unbelief, sin, and disaster, it is never too late for God to deal triumphantly with these tragic facts if brought to Him in full surrender and trust.

TO MAKE, NOT BREAK

*Thou hast shewed thy
people hard things.*
Psalms 60:3

The tests of life are to make, not break us.

A DEEP REST

Be still, and know that I am God.
Psalms 46:10

There is for the heart that will cease from itself, a deep rest which the world can neither give nor take away.

PRAY THROUGH

Take the arrows ... Smite upon the ground. And he smote thrice and stayed. And the man of God was wroth with him, and said, Thou shouldest have smitten five or six times.
2 Kings 13:18-19

How important that we should learn to pray through!

SPRINGS OF WATER

And Caleb said unto her, What wouldest thou? Who answered, Give me a blessing; for thou hast given me a south land; give me also springs of water. And he gave her the upper springs, and the nether springs.
Joshua 15:18-19

How many and how precious these springs, and how much more there is to be possessed of God's own fullness!

THE IMPOSSIBLE

*For with God nothing
shall be impossible.*
Luke 1:37

We love to see the impossible done. And so does God. Let faith swing out to Him. He is the God of the impossible.

REJOICE!

Thou makest the outgoings of the morning and evening to rejoice.
Psalms 65:8

In the holy hush of the early dawn
I hear a Voice –
I am with you all the day,
Rejoice! Rejoice!

THE AFTERWARD

Nevertheless afterward.
Hebrews 12:11

You can always count on God to make the "afterward" of difficulties, if rightly overcome, a thousand times richer and fairer than the forward.

SEEK THEM NOT

And seekest thou great things for thyself? seek them not: for, behold, I will bring evil upon all flesh, saith the Lord: but thy life will I give unto thee for a prey in all places whither thou goest.

Jeremiah 45:5

Lord, give me my life for a prey, and in the hardest places help me today to be victorious.

DECEMBER

A REST TO THE PEOPLE

*There remaineth therefore a
rest to the people of God.*
Hebrews 4:9

"**M**y dear child, I did not give you
these loads; you have no need of them.
Just drop them, and you will find the
path easy and you will be as if borne
on eagle's wings."

SUFFERING

Perfect through sufferings.
Hebrews 2:10

Suffering is a wonderful fertilizer to the roots of character.

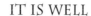

IT IS WELL

Is it well with thy husband? Is it well with the child? And she answered, It is well.
2 Kings 4:26

Afflictions cannot injure when blended with submission.

ONLY GOD ENTERS

He went up into a mountain apart.
Matthew 14:23

Every life that would be strong must have its Holy of Holies into which only God enters.

FOLLOW WHERE
HE LEADS

Teach me thy way, O LORD,
and lead me in a plain path.
Psalms 27:11

Many people want to direct God, instead of resigning themselves to be directed by Him; to show Him a way, instead of passively following where He leads.

I COME QUICKLY

*Behold, I come quickly: hold
that fast which thou hast, that
no man take thy crown.*
Revelation 3:11

Ought I not to do what I can for the
Lord Jesus while He tarries, and to
rouse a slumbering church?

OH, FOR THAT FAITH

*Ye shall not see wind, neither shall ye
see rain; yet that valley shall be filled
with water, that ye may drink, both
ye, and your cattle, and your beasts.*
2 Kings 3:16

Oh, for that faith that can act by faith
and not by sight, and expect God to
work although we see no wind or rain.

KINDNESS

*Put on ... as the elect
of God ... kindness.*
Colossians 3:12

A word spoken pleasantly is a large spot of sunshine on a sad heart. Therefore, "Give others the sunshine, tell Jesus the rest."

A WEIGHT OF GLORY

*For this our light and transitory
burden of suffering is achieving
for us a weight of glory.*
2 Corinthians 4:17

It is comforting to know that sorrow
tarries only for the night; it takes its
leave in the morning. A thunderstorm
is very brief when put alongside the
long summer day.

SHARE THE SUFFERINGS AND COMFORT

*As you share the sufferings
you share the comfort also.*
2 Corinthians 1:7

Do not fret, or set your teeth, or wait doggedly for the suffering to pass; but get out of it all you can, both for yourself and for your service to your generation, according to the will of God.

DECEMBER 11

IN GOD'S HOUSE
BY NIGHT

*Ye servants of the LORD, which by
night stand in the house of the LORD.
The LORD that made heaven and
earth bless thee out of Zion.*
Psalms 134:1, 3

To stand in God's house by night, to
worship in the depth of sorrow –
therein lies the blessing; it is the test of
perfect faith.

DECEMBER 12

I HAVE KEPT THE FAITH

*The last drops of my sacrifice
are falling; my time to go has
come. I have fought a good
fight; I have kept the faith.*
2 Timothy 4:6-7

God will not look you over for medals, degrees of diplomas, but for scars.

THE MOST EXQUISITE

I will give thee the treasures of darkness.
Isaiah 45:3

If we are faithful and fail not and faint not, we shall some day know that the most exquisite work of all our life was done in those days when it was so dark.

CHRIST'S FORETHOUGHT

*His disciples said unto him,
Lord, teach us to pray ... and he
said unto them, When ye pray,
say ... Thy kingdom come.*
Luke 11:1-2

The missionary enterprise is not the church's afterthought; it is Christ's forethought.

TRUST!

Trust also in him.
Psalms 37:5

Trust! The way will open, the right issue will come, the end will be peace, the cloud will be lifted, and the light of eternal noonday shall shine at last.

DECEMBER 16

PERSEVERANCE
IN PRAYER

*And there was Anna, a prophetess
... which departed not from the
temple, but served God with
fastings and prayers night and day.*
Luke 2:36-37

No doubt by praying we learn to
pray, and the more we pray the oftener
we can pray, and the better we can
pray. Perseverance in prayer is necessary to prevalence in prayer.

DECEMBER 17

GOD OF PEACE

And the very God of peace sanctify you wholly; and I pray God your whole spirit and soul and body be preserved blameless unto the coming of our Lord Jesus Christ. Faithful is he that calleth you, who also will do it.
1 Thessalonians 5:23-24

Holiness makes the soul like a field or garden of God, with all manner of pleasant fruits and flowers.

MORE THAN CONQUERORS

In all these things we are more than conquerors through him that loved us.
Romans 8:37

To be more than conqueror is to take the spoils from the enemy and appropriate them to yourself.

DECEMBER 19

FOR A TESTIMONY

It shall turn to you for a testimony.
Luke 21:13

Life is a steep climb, and it does the heart good to have somebody "call back" and cheerily beckon us on up the high hill.

WALK ALONE WITH GOD

*Yet I am not alone, because
the Father is with me.*
John 16:32

The life that is lived unto God, however it forfeits human companionships, knows divine fellowship. No man ever comes into a realization of the best things of God, who does not learn to walk alone with God.

DECEMBER 21

EVERY DUTY HAS
A BLESSING

*To him will I give the land that
he hath trodden upon ... because
he hath wholly followed the Lord.*
Deuteronomy 1:36

Every hard duty that lies in your path
has a blessing in it. Not to do it, at
whatever cost, is to miss the blessing.

ABANDON TO GOD

*Lo, an horror of great
darkness fell upon him.*
Genesis 15:12

Never should we so abandon ourselves to God as when He seems to have abandoned us.

I WILL REFRESH YOU

The journey is too great for thee.
1 Kings 19:7

Hear the words of the Master: "I am going to refresh you."

SPEND TIME MEDITATING

And Isaac went out to meditate in the field at the eventide.
Genesis 24:63

We should be better Christians if we were more alone; we should do more if we attempted less, and spent more time in retirement, and quiet waiting upon God.

GOD WITH US

His name shall be called
Emmanuel ... God with us.
Matthew 1:23

O come, all ye faithful,
joyful and triumphant.
O come ye, O come ye
to Bethlehem;
Come and behold Him,
born the King of Angels,
O come let us adore Him,
Christ, the Lord.

SIT YE HERE

Sit ye here, while I go and pray yonder.
Matthew 26:36

It is a hard thing to be kept in the background at a time of crisis. Remember it is Christ that says, "Sit ye here."

THE IRON CROWN

His soul entered into iron.
Psalms 105:18

The iron crown of suffering precedes the golden crown of glory. And iron is entering into your soul to make it strong and brave.

ALWAYS REJOICE

*Rejoice in the Lord always:
and again I say, Rejoice.*
Philippians 4:4

Sing across the winter snow,
Pierce the cloud;
Sing when mists are drooping low –
Clear and loud;
But sing sweetest in the dark;
He who slumbers not will hark.

APPROPRIATING FAITH

Arise ... enter to possess the land ... for God hath given it into your hands; a place where there is no want of any thing that is in the earth.
Judges 18:9-10

We need to have appropriating faith in regard to God's promises. We must make God's Word our own personal possession.

Teachers

Make the Difference

Introduction

The book you hold in your hands is
an expression of gratitude.

Thank you for helping me learn, for
inspiring me in some way, for making
me rethink what I thought to be true,
for teaching me to challenge ideas
instead of simply accepting them,
and for helping me think for myself.

You have truly made a difference.

—C. G.

*To unlock
the intellect, the
imagination
is key.*

To teach well one must
be part clown, part actor,
part drill sergeant, part
friend, and part parent.

abcdefghijklmnop

Learning occurs
within the student,
not within the
classroom.

abcdefghijklmnop

For every class clown to tolerate there is a genius in the making.

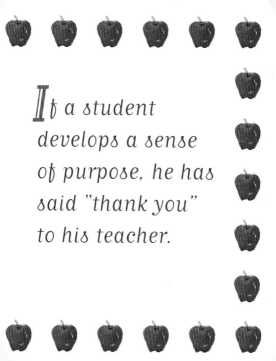

If a student develops a sense of purpose, he has said "thank you" to his teacher.

Teachers inspire
students to dream,
and give them the tools
and knowledge to make
those dreams possible.

While teaching in front
of a class of students,
a teacher is also
standing behind them.

Often it's teaching
how to think,
not what to think,
that's important.

Someone who can
make you believe in
things that are intangible
has a rare gift for
expression. Teachers
do that every day.

abcdefghijklmnop

An educator does not
make a test easy.
An educator inspires a
child so that the difficult
becomes interesting.

abcdefghijklmnop

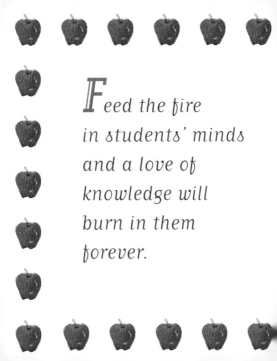

Feed the fire in students' minds and a love of knowledge will burn in them forever.

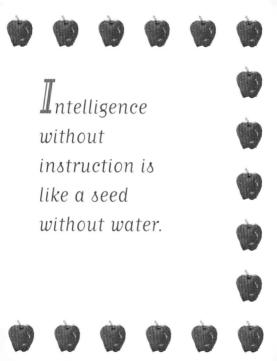

Intelligence without instruction is like a seed without water.

Treat children as
if they are ignorant,
and they
will remain so.

To teach is
the easiest
way to learn.

A person who can
spark a love of learning
in you is more than just
a teacher. That person
is a true mentor.

*Nothing inspires
a student more than
a teacher who is
in love with his or
her subject.*

The teacher who takes the time and has the patience to connect with a troubled child is never forgotten.

Teachers teach not
only a subject or a class,
but also valuable
lessons that may not
be understood until
later in life.

abcdefghijklmnop

For every former
student who returns
to say "thank you,"
there are 100 who have
said "thanks" in
their hearts.

abcdefghijklmnop

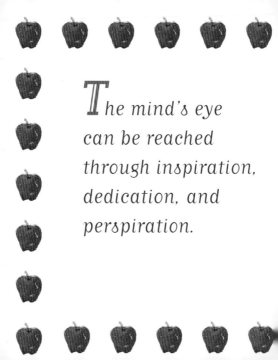

The mind's eye can be reached through inspiration, dedication, and perspiration.

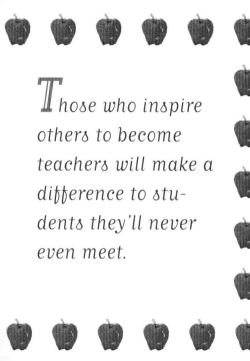

Those who inspire others to become teachers will make a difference to students they'll never even meet.

Sometimes it takes years for the wisdom of a particular teacher to sink in. That doesn't make the lesson any less important than those learned immediately.

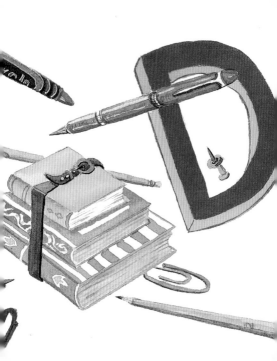

A good teacher not
only teaches the curriculum,
but also continues to deepen
her own knowledge as she
introduces her students
to a subject.

Teachers who can
entertain as well as educate,
who make even the most
boring lessons fun, are those
who inspire the love of
learning for a lifetime.

Learning is made easier through encouragement.

A challenge given will always be met.

A teacher must
form a bond with a
student during the school
year; a teacher who
has truly inspired a
student has formed
a lifetime bond.

Love of learning is contagious. There is no student, however untutored, whom a wise teacher cannot reach.

abcdefghijklmnop

In the classroom of a well-liked teacher, "June" is a four-letter word spoken with regret.

abcdefghijklmnop

At some point, the student realizes that his best teachers weren't just teachers; they were friends who brought out the best in him.

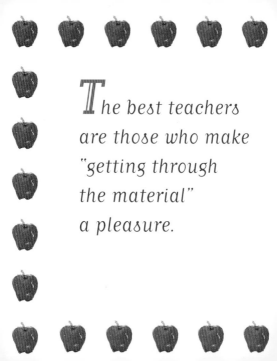

The best teachers are those who make "getting through the material" a pleasure.

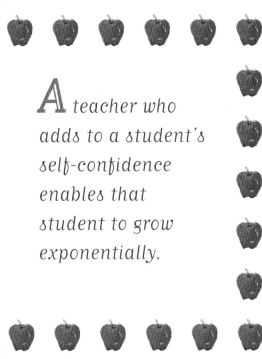

A teacher who adds to a student's self-confidence enables that student to grow exponentially.

Shakespeare inspired
his entire audience from
queen to moneylender
to fishwife. A teacher
does the same.

It is a miracle to inspire
students to think on their
own and to speak their minds,
no matter how contrary to
popular thought. Never stop
believing in miracles.

Teaching is a living art. The master teacher seeks new methods, learning from her students.

A teacher doesn't need
to have a classroom
to be a teacher.
Those who inspire and
help us grow are the
unsung educators.

A true teacher

never stops

learning.

Learning by rote is
simple memorization;
anyone can do that.
Self-sufficiency comes
with learning through
example and inspiration.

a b c d e f g h i j k l m n o p

Dreamers, idealists,
and teachers all show
us what is possible with
a little sense of pride and
a lot of hard work.

abcdefghijklmnop

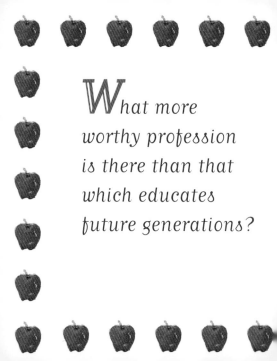

*W*hat more worthy profession is there than that which educates future generations?

Keep your eyes
on the future,
your mind in the
present, and stay
in touch with
the past.

Great tutors cost
a pretty penny, but
those untutored pay
a heavy price.

The mind is not just a
sponge that soaks up
knowledge; it is a seed
that sprouts and gives
life to other seeds.

The smart man
learns from others,
the wise man from
his own mistakes.

Many are taught but few actually learn.

The worth of a
good teacher is
often more
evident after
she retires.

Learning is a privilege,
but teaching is a
greater one.

a b c d e f g h i j k l m n o p

A successful teacher
not only recognizes
talent but also helps
create it.

abcdefghijklmnop

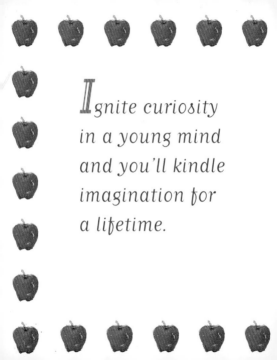

*I*gnite curiosity
in a young mind
and you'll kindle
imagination for
a lifetime.

The most important thing you can impart to a child is a wish to learn.

You never know when a student will recognize something in a lesson that the teacher hasn't seen. Even the wisest of scholars can learn from a pupil.

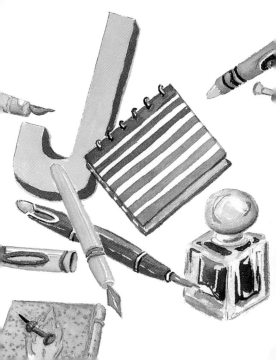

Keep the lesson entertaining and it will lessen the need for discipline.

Teachers must be
able to instruct the
individual while
keeping track of the
entire class.

It is easier to track a student's test scores than his inner development. Scores, however, are mere indicators of the real growth within.

The most
expensive thing
in the world
is ignorance.

Educators plant
their feet in front
of a class and
start cultivating
young minds.

abcdefghijklmnop

To say you have taught
when no one has learned
is like saying you have
written when your
pen is out of ink.

abcdefghijklmnop

You never know what combination of words will unlock a child's growth.

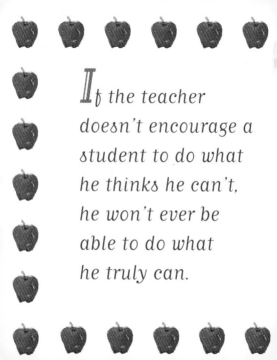

If the teacher doesn't encourage a student to do what he thinks he can't, he won't ever be able to do what he truly can.

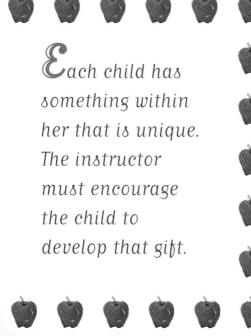

Each child has something within her that is unique. The instructor must encourage the child to develop that gift.

Building monuments
celebrates what is now;
building young minds
creates the future.

Optimism and pessimism
are both catching.
A great teacher exhibits
the first, and avoids the
second like the plague.

Children are great mimics. Show them how to do something and they'll want to do it too. Tell them, and they'll sit back and watch.

To reach a child,
bend down to
his level.
To inspire him,
stand back up.

We all possess a capacity for learning— and a potential for it that is never fully realized.